WOMEN WHO DARE

Women of the Suffrage Movement

BY

JANICE E. RUTH & EVELYN SINCLAIR

Pomegranate

SAN FRANCISCO

LIBRARY OF CONGRESS
WASHINGTON, DC

Published by Pomegranate Communications, Inc.
Box 808022, Petaluma CA 94975
800 227 1428; www.pomegranate.com

Pomegranate Europe Ltd.
Unit 1, Heathcote Business Centre, Hurlbutt Road
Warwick, Warwickshire CV34 6TD, UK
[+44] 0 1926 430111; sales@pomeurope.co.uk

Amy Pastan, Series Editor

In association with the Library of Congress, Pomegranate publishes other books in the Women Who
Dare® series, as well as calendars, books of postcards, posters, and Knowledge Cards® featuring daring
women. Please contact the publisher for more information.

Library of Congress Cataloging-in-Publication Data

Ruth, Janice E.
      Women of the suffrage movement / by Janice E. Ruth & Evelyn Sinclair.
         p. cm. — (Women who dare)
      Includes bibliographical references.
      ISBN 0-7649-3547-X
      1. Suffragists—United States—Biography. 2. Suffragists—United States—History. 3. Women—
Suffrage—United States—History. I. Title. II. Women who dare (Petaluma, Calif.)

   JK1898.5.R88 2006
   324.6'23092273—dc22

                                                                                    2005040190

Pomegranate Catalog No. A113
Designed by Harrah Lord, Yellow House Studio, Rockport ME
Printed in Korea

15 14 13 12 11 10 09 08 07 06   10 9 8 7 6 5 4 3 2 1

FRONT COVER: Automobiles symbolized women's independence, transported activists across large dis-
tances, and provided effective speaking platforms for suffrage organizers such as Margaret Foley, who
addressed crowds in Cleveland, Ohio, in May 1912.
NAWSA RECORDS, MANUSCRIPT DIVISION. LC-MSS-34132-5

BACK COVER: Elizabeth Cady Stanton (1815–1902) and Susan B. Anthony (1820–1906), shown here in the
1870s, worked side by side for more than fifty years, their loyalty to one another and to the suffrage
cause surviving differences of opinion and personality.
NWP RECORDS, MANUSCRIPT DIVISION. LC-MSS-34355-36

PREFACE

FOR TWO HUNDRED YEARS, the Library of Congress, the oldest national cultural institution in the United States, has been gathering materials necessary to tell the stories of women in America. The last third of the twentieth century witnessed a great surge of popular and scholarly interest in women's studies and women's history that has led to an outpouring of works in many formats. Drawing on women's history resources in the collections of the Library of Congress, the Women Who Dare book series is designed to provide readers with an entertaining introduction to the life of a notable American woman or a significant topic in women's history.

From its beginnings in 1800 as a legislative library, the Library of Congress has grown into a national library that houses both a universal collection of knowledge and the mint record of American creativity. Congress' decision to purchase Thomas Jefferson's personal library to replace the books and maps burned during the British occupation in 1814 set the Congressional Library on the path of collecting with the breadth of Jefferson's interests. Not just American imprints were to be acquired, but foreign-language materials as well, and Jefferson's library already included works by American and European women.

The Library of Congress has some 121 million items, largely housed in closed stacks in three buildings on Capitol Hill that contain twenty public reading rooms. The incredible, wide-ranging collections include books, maps, prints, newspapers, broadsides, diaries, letters, posters, musical scores, photographs, audio and video recordings, and documents available only in digital formats. The Library serves first-time users and the most experienced researchers alike.

I hope that you, the reader, will seek and find in the pages of this book information that will further your understanding of women's history. In addition, I hope you will continue to explore the topic of this book in a library near you, in person at the Library of Congress, or by visiting the Library on the World Wide Web at http://www.loc.gov. Happy reading!

—JAMES H. BILLINGTON, The Librarian of Congress

■ As more women began to move out of the home and into public spaces, they organized suffrage parades, beginning in California and Iowa in 1908, with the first large event occurring in New York in 1910. Suffragists often brought their children and infants to parades, such as this one on May 6, 1912, in New York City, demonstrating that mothers needed the vote. LC-USZC4-5585

The largest reform movement in American history—the campaign for women's right to vote—lasted more than seventy years. During that time, determined women assembled, argued, petitioned, lobbied, paraded, picketed, and even went to jail for daring to support suffrage. Women's demand for the vote was radical and transforming. The campaign questioned the country's commitment to democracy, highlighted persistent racial and class tensions, and challenged existing domestic relationships. It also personally affected—for better and worse—the women and families who became involved in the struggle. Their story is one of hope and perseverance, fortitude, skill, sacrifice, courage, and conviction. Sadly, few of the women who began the suffrage campaign before the Civil War lived long enough to witness its final victory—ratification of the Nineteenth Amendment in August 1920—but their work was carried on by the younger women they inspired and taught.

Family ties and personal associations nurtured a network of suffrage supporters that grew into local, state, and national organizations. Suffrage leader Anna Howard Shaw recalled that if any state in the South was not organized for the suffrage campaign, it must be because "no family there had three sisters to start the movement." Eventually millions of American women were involved, keeping the issue alive not only in the halls of Congress and at the White House gates, but in state legislatures, on the

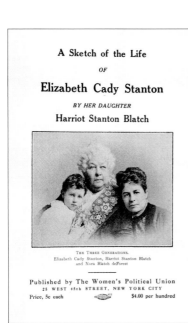

A Sketch of the Life

OF

Elizabeth Cady Stanton

BY HER DAUGHTER

Harriot Stanton Blatch

THE THREE GENERATIONS,
Elizabeth Cady Stanton, Harriot Stanton Blatch
and Nora Blatch deForest

Published by The Women's Political Union
25 WEST 45th STREET, NEW YORK CITY
Price, 5c each $4.00 per hundred

■ *Suffrage daughters, like Harriot Stanton Blatch, Alice Stone Blackwell, Anne Fitzhugh Miller, Sue Shelton White, and others, lovingly wrote tributes about their mothers' accomplishments. This sketch, published for the centennial of Elizabeth Cady Stanton's birth in 1915, illustrates the commitment to suffrage across three generations: Stanton, her daughter, and her granddaughter.*

HARRIOT STANTON BLATCH PAPERS,
MANUSCRIPT DIVISION. LC-MSS-12997-22

front pages of daily newspapers, and in family parlors and dining rooms everywhere.

A meeting in Seneca Falls, New York, in 1848 marked the beginning of the movement. Its organizers—Elizabeth Cady Stanton, Lucretia Mott, her sister Martha C. Wright, and Mott's fellow Quakers Jane Hunt and Mary McClintock—were not, as Stanton noted, "the sour old maids, childless women, nor divorced wives . . . the newspapers declared them to be." All were married and had children, and they ranged in age from thirty-two to fifty-four. They were influenced by the work of Frances Wright, Sarah and Angelina Grimké, Lydia Maria Child, and especially Mary Wollstonecraft.

Written in 1792, Mary Wollstonecraft's *Vindication of the Rights of Woman* introduced the concept of women's rights to eighteenth- and nineteenth-century women in both America and her native Britain, where women had no legal status after marriage. Women could not sign contracts, hold title to their own earnings and property, obtain divorces easily, or gain custody of children after divorce. Stanton's good friend Susan B. Anthony hung Wollstonecraft's picture on a wall in her home, and Anthony and Stanton serialized *A Vindication of the Rights of Woman* in the suffrage newspaper they published in the early 1870s.

More than three hundred men and women assembled in Seneca Falls for the purpose of discussing "the social, civil, and religious condition and rights of women." Stanton later recalled that she and her friends, with no experience planning a meeting, "felt as helpless and hopeless as if they had been suddenly asked to construct a steam engine," and they asked a man, Lucretia's husband, James Mott, to call the meeting to order. In the course of the two-day convention, Stanton's "Declaration of Rights and Sentiments" was read and adopted. Modeled after the Declaration of Independence, it protested women's inferior legal status and put forward a list of eleven proposals for the moral, economic, and political equality of women. The most radical resolution, the demand that women have the right to vote, was the only one that did not pass unanimously, surviving only because Stanton and former slave Frederick Douglass spoke so eloquently for its passage.

Women's rights conventions became annual events, and the first

■ *In the decade following the first women's rights meeting in Seneca Falls, New York, the conventions that were held throughout the North and the West often received unsympathetic reports in the press. On June 11, 1859, the New York–based newspaper* Harper's Weekly *published a wood engraving mocking the annual conventions.* LC-USZ62-2036

national meeting in October 1850 drew supporters from New York, Massachusetts, New Hampshire, Vermont, Ohio, Pennsylvania, Iowa, and California to Worcester, Massachusetts, the site selected by its principal organizer, Paulina Wright Davis. Lucy Stone and her future sisters-in-law—Antoinette Brown and Marianne and Sarah Ellen Blackwell—attended, as did Vermont newspaper editor Clarina Howard Nichols, pioneer physician Harriot K. Hunt, women's property rights advocate Ernestine Rose, and many leading abolitionists, including Lucretia Mott, Mariana and Oliver Johnson, Parker and Sarah Pillsbury, Frederick Douglass, and Sojourner Truth.

At national and state meetings throughout the 1850s, participants discussed women's educational opportunities, divorce reform, property rights, and sometimes equal wages and shorter work hours for women. From these meetings, women went out to petition state legislatures to change unfair laws. They made speeches, some quite memorable, such as former slave Sojourner Truth's "Ain't I a Woman?" address in Akron, Ohio. They also wrote letters, published articles, and constantly argued for their beliefs.

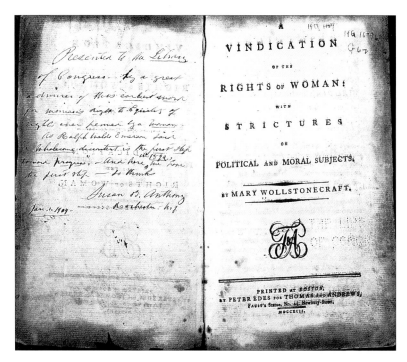

■ *In her copy of* A Vindication of the Rights of Woman *(1792), which she donated to the Library of Congress in 1904, Susan B. Anthony identified herself as "a great admirer of this earliest work for women's right to Equality of rights," by Mary Wollstonecraft.*

Family and Friends
Elizabeth Smith Miller (1822–1911)
and Anne Fitzhugh Miller (1856–1912)

Even before Elizabeth Smith Miller was born, her family home in Peterboro, New York, was a center of hospitality and political discussion in the community. Her father, Gerrit Smith, was an ardent abolitionist, and the Smith mansion became a station on the Underground Railroad. Her father's cousin, Elizabeth Cady, visited often, and the two girls spent one afternoon in 1837 in the attic, listening to fugitive Harriet Powell's accounts of growing up in slavery. In October 1839 Elizabeth Cady met abolitionist Henry Stanton at the Smiths'; she married him in May 1840.

In 1843 Elizabeth Smith married banker Charles Dudley Miller. Both Elizabeth and her husband signed the call that was sent out to invite participants to the first national women's rights convention in Worcester in 1850. As a mother of young children and a woman who loved to garden, Elizabeth adopted a practical form of dress: a shorter skirt over loose trousers, which resembled clothing worn during water-cure treatments. Her cousin Elizabeth Cady Stanton and Stanton's neighbor Amelia Bloomer promptly copied Miller's design. Bloomer publicized it in her temperance newspaper, The Lily, *and it became known as the bloomer outfit. Elizabeth Cady Stanton was wearing bloomers in March 1851 when her neighbor introduced her to her houseguest Susan B. Anthony, beginning the fifty-year Stanton-Anthony friendship and a powerful partnership in the suffrage campaign.*

When Gerrit Smith served in Congress in 1852–1853, Elizabeth Smith Miller accompanied her father to Washington and discovered that her bloomer outfit was

■ *"My street dress was a dark brown corded silk, short skirt and straight trousers, a short but graceful and richly trimmed French cloak of black velvet with drooping sleeves,"* wrote Elizabeth Smith Miller of the outfit she designed for herself in the spring of 1851. Both her father and her husband supported her in embracing dress reform, but jeers in the street and a critical press led her to abandon it after several years.

less conspicuous and less subject to ridicule in the larger city. But by the time Miller's only daughter, Anne Fitzhugh Miller, was born in 1856, Elizabeth was again wearing more fashionable clothing, having realized that the dress question was distracting people from more important issues, such as advanced education for women.

Anne grew up with three older brothers and was educated at home in Peterboro. In 1869, the family moved to Lochland, a lakeside estate in Geneva, New York, that would become a meeting place for suffragists. A year earlier, her mother, with others, had petitioned the Republican convention in Chicago to add women's suffrage to the party's platform, but without success.

At age nineteen, Anne, her mother, and her friend Ruth Leslie VerPlanck started a camp on the opposite side of Seneca Lake from the family home. Camp Fossenvue became a summer retreat for reformers and suffragists of either sex who enjoyed camping, swimming, and philosophical, political, and literary debate. Susan B. Anthony, her sister Mary, and Elizabeth Cady Stanton spent restful August weeks there. Alice Stone Blackwell arrived there by lake steamer for her first visit in August 1901.

Elizabeth Smith Miller, a lifelong financial supporter of women's rights, provided lodging at Lochland for the state suffrage association's annual meeting, held in Geneva in October 1897. The next month, Elizabeth and Anne organized the Geneva Political Equality Club; from 1898 to 1911, daughter Anne was its president and her mother its honorary president. The two began keeping scrapbooks of club events, documenting suffrage activities. Noted suffrage speakers came to lecture. Harriet Tubman stayed at Lochland, attended meetings, and was made a lifetime member of the club.

In 1906 and 1908, Anne testified at US Senate hearings on a suffrage

■ On the veranda at Lochland, Elizabeth Smith Miller and her daughter Anne Fitzhugh Miller hosted an annual piazza party, here probably in May 1909, for the Geneva Political Equality Club, which they had founded in 1897. ELIZABETH SMITH MILLER AND ANNE FITZHUGH MILLER SCRAPBOOKS, RARE BOOK AND SPECIAL COLLECTIONS DIVISION

amendment. In 1910, Elizabeth became ill, and Anne retired to care for her mother until her death the next year. Then in 1912, Anne died suddenly in a Boston hotel while on a suffrage trip. Waiting at home in Geneva was a bright green parrot who could cry, "Votes for women." Anne had intended to carry the bird on her shoulder in the May 1912 suffrage parade in New York City.

■ Former slave Harriet Tubman (c. 1820–1913), photographed probably around 1911 at her home in Auburn, New York, held a life membership in the Geneva Political Equality Club.

■ Beginning with the Kansas state suffrage referendum in 1867, the sunflower—the state symbol—and the color gold or yellow became associated with the suffrage cause. Banners, sashes, buttons, and delegates' ribbons, such as this one collected by the Millers from the 1899 National American Woman Suffrage Association convention, were chiefly yellow.

DELEGATE

N.A.W.S.A.

31st ANNUAL

CONVENTION

April 27...
... to ...'
May 3, '99

GRAND RAPIDS, MICH.

■ *In 1886 Lucy Stone and Henry Blackwell invited aging abolitionists to a reunion at their home in Boston. Present were Elizabeth Buffum Chace, Sarah Southwick, Abby Kelley Foster, Lucy Stone, and Zilpha Spooner* (seated on porch); *Francis Garrison, Alla Foster, and George Garrison* (standing on porch); *and Samuel May, William Lloyd Garrison Jr., Harriet Sewall, Samuel Sewall, Wendell Garrison, Henry Blackwell, and Theodore Weld* (front row). NAWSA RECORDS, MANUSCRIPT DIVISION. LC-MSS-34132-6

ELIZABETH SMITH MILLER, Lucy Stone, Susan B. Anthony, and other early suffragists had learned to organize, hold public meetings, raise money, and conduct successful petition drives in the temperance and abolition movements. They also had gained experience with hostile audiences and had begun to develop a political philosophy. As early as the 1830s, South Carolinian abolitionists Angelina and Sarah Grimké began to link the issues of slavery and women's status. When the abolitionist movement split into two organizations in May 1839, the wing led by William Lloyd Garrison supported women's full participation, and the wing led by Lewis Tappan limited women's involvement to female auxiliaries. The debate about gender roles in the antislavery movement was coupled with a similar debate about whether white and black abolitionists should work together or separately.

Immediately after the Civil War, Americans focused on three new amendments to the US Constitution. Women worked for the Thirteenth Amendment abolishing slavery, believing that a universal suffrage amendment would follow, but both the Fourteenth and Fifteenth Amendments ignored women's demand for full citizenship. The Fourteenth Amendment promised all *male* citizens over the age of twenty-one the right to vote, inserting the first mention of sex in the Constitution. Lucy Stone, Julia Ward Howe, and others accepted the idea that this was "the Negro's hour" and supported passage of the amendments, but Anthony and Stanton opposed them because they failed to include women. The former allies split into two groups, forcing friends and acquaintances to choose sides in 1869.

■ *As Uncle Sam laughs in the background, Susan B. Anthony—a good target for cartoonists—chases President Grover Cleveland with a "woman suffrage" umbrella. Cleveland steadfastly ignored women's demand to vote, though he nonetheless appreciated the support of women's clubs in his presidential campaigns of 1884 and 1892.*

DIGITAL ID: acd 2a05652

Stanton and Anthony formed the National Woman Suffrage Association (NWSA) specifically to press for a federal amendment enfranchising women. Howe, Stone, and Stone's husband, Henry Browne Blackwell, formed the competing American Woman Suffrage Association (AWSA), which advocated state-by-state enfranchisement of women. AWSA focused on women's suffrage and avoided NWSA's efforts to link it to issues such as trade unionism and divorce reform.

FAMILY VALUES
LUCY STONE (1818–1893) AND ALICE STONE BLACKWELL (1857–1950)

*From the time she was a young woman growing up in West Brookfield,
Massachusetts, Lucy Stone was keenly interested in women's rights and wanted
as good an education as her brothers received. She first entered Mount Holyoke
College, but not taking to sex-segregated education, she switched to Oberlin College
in Ohio, where she financed her studies through paid work and earned a degree in
1847. At Oberlin she met Antoinette Brown, who would become an ordained minister as well as Stone's lifelong friend, sister-in-law, and fellow campaigner for
women's rights.*

    *A skilled public speaker, Lucy Stone lectured against slavery and for women,
but it was the desire for women's rights that impassioned her. Stone wore the
bloomer outfit popularized in* The Lily *and became a model for other women who
welcomed the freedom of wearing pants. Reluctant to marry, she was courted persis-
tently by Henry Browne Blackwell, an abolitionist merchant, and in 1855 she married him. Stone stopped wearing bloomers, which Blackwell did not like, but the
couple fashioned an original marriage agreement that gave her control of her own
property. After consulting lawyers, Stone kept her maiden name. In this, too, she
became a model for others; women who kept their own names were henceforth
called "Lucy Stoners."*

    *Lucy Stone was thirty-nine years old when her daughter, Alice, was born.
Alice, a lively and smart student, spent her teenage years in Boston and met many
of her parents' suffragist friends at home and at the offices of the* Woman's
Journal, *which Stone and Blackwell founded in 1870 to speak for the women's*

■ *A daguerreotype shows Lucy Stone holding her three-month-old daughter, Alice, born September 14, 1857, and raised in the midst of her parents' many suffrage activities and friendships.* BLACKWELL FAMILY PAPERS, MANUSCRIPT DIVISION. LC-MSS-12880-25

movement. After a meeting of the New England Woman's Suffrage Association in May 1872, Alice expressed her opinion, privately in her personal journal, of Abigail Scott Duniway from Oregon: "When the Editress of the New North West, a lady I don't like at all, began to speak, I retreated to the dressing room, and waited, sleepy and thirsty, till the meeting was over." In December 1873, she wrote of Susan B. Anthony, "I don't much like Miss A. She strikes me as being tall, sharp, dictatorial, conceited, pugnacious & selfish. Also plucky, undoubtedly."

Alice Stone Blackwell graduated from Boston University and in 1884 became an editor of the Woman's Journal, a job she held until 1917. Putting aside their families' past differences, she and Harriot Stanton Blatch helped unite their mothers' competing suffrage organizations in 1890 as the National American Woman Suffrage Association; Blackwell served as its secretary for twenty years. She was active in the Women's Trade Union League, National Association for the Advancement of Colored People, and American Peace Society. Blackwell and her friend Ohannes Chatschumian, a theology student from Leipzig, established Friends of Armenia. Translating Armenian poetry with Chatschumian, who died in 1896, Blackwell became interested in world poetry and international human rights. One of her ongoing literary projects was a biography of her mother, Lucy Stone: Pioneer of Woman's Rights (1930), a work of love that took her many years to complete.

■ *Alice Stone Blackwell (left) edits the* Woman's Journal *outdoors in the company of Anna Howard Shaw (1847–1919) in 1896. Shaw, a national lecturer for the National American Woman Suffrage Association, became its president in 1904, remaining in office until 1915.* BLACKWELL FAMILY PAPERS, MANUSCRIPT DIVISION. LC-MSS-12880-26

■ *Frances E. Willard (1839–1898), who turned the Woman's Christian Temperance Union into a powerful force for reform, represents American women in Henrietta Briggs-Wall's 1893 image showing women classed politically with idiots, convicts, the insane, and American Indians, none of whom could vote. A member of the Kansas Equal Suffrage Association, Briggs-Wall exhibited this picture at the 1893 World's Columbian Exposition in Chicago.*

SUFFRAGE LEADERS STONE, Howe, Anthony, and Stanton swept across the country giving suffrage talks in the late 1860s and 1870s. Their visits often inspired the creation of new suffrage organizations or attracted members to existing groups. Key leaders emerged in every region, including Abigail Scott Duniway, editor of the *New Northwest;* minister Olympia Brown in Wisconsin; Mary Jackman Colburn and Martha Rogers Ripley, both medical doctors, in Minnesota; journalists Caroline Nichols Churchill and Ellis Meredith in Colorado; and Esther Hobart Morris, a justice of the peace in Wyoming. A flurry of state work achieved partial voting rights for women on bond measures, tax issues, and municipal and school board elections.

Other reform organizations helped build backing for suffrage. The Woman's Christian Temperance Union (WCTU), formed in 1874, quickly became the nation's largest women's organization under the leadership of Frances Willard. White and black women formed segregated local branches and helped spread the suffrage message into the West, expanding the WCTU's mission of closing saloons to undertake prison reform, public health awareness, and better working conditions for women.

In 1878 Senator Aaron Augustus Sargent of California introduced the first federal women's suffrage amendment. After active lobbying by suffragists, committee hearings were held in 1882 and every few years thereafter throughout the 1880s and 1890s. The first time the amendment emerged from committee to be considered on the Senate or House floor was in 1886; during the subsequent vote in January 1887, only 50 of 76 senators even bothered to vote, defeating the amendment 34 to 16. The amendment would not be voted on again until 1914. Major opponents included midwestern liquor interests, southern conservatives who wanted to protect their region's de facto disenfranchisement of black men, and eastern business leaders who relied on child labor and unregulated hours and working conditions.

Suffragists pressed their case in courts of law and in the court of public opinion. In the presidential election of 1872, Susan B. Anthony tried to vote in Rochester, New York, and Virginia Louisa Minor in Missouri. When Minor was refused a ballot by election official Reese Happersett, her husband took her case to the US Supreme Court, arguing that Missouri law limiting the vote to men was in violation of her rights as a citizen under the Fifteenth Amendment. When the Court ruled against her in *Minor v. Happersett* (1874), it reaffirmed the right of states to establish suffrage qualifications.

By the end of the 1880s, the women's rights movement was becoming more conservative and more racist. Earlier, women had argued for universal suffrage on the basis of the individual rights of all people, regardless of sex and race. Starting in the 1870s, however, suffragists began to claim that women should be given the vote because they were different from men, and their distinctly higher morals would uplift the nation. This emphasis on character and qualifications widened the gaps between suffragists created by differences in class, race, education, or place of birth. Organizations nevertheless sprang up to include women with vastly different backgrounds and goals in the campaign.

In 1890, Alice Stone Blackwell and Harriot Stanton Blatch helped to

■ *Early in 1871, Victoria Woodhull (1838–1927), who ran for US president in 1872, and other suffragists lobbied the House of Representatives Judiciary Committee, arguing that women's right to vote was inherent in the Fourteenth and Fifteenth Amendments. The event was reported in* Frank Leslie's Illustrated Newspaper. LC-USZ62-2023

broker the merger of the two major national organizations, which put aside many of their differences to become the National American Woman Suffrage Association (NAWSA). The *Woman's Journal,* the weekly newspaper that Blackwell and her parents continued to edit, became its voice. Ironically, although NAWSA's headquarters and many of its national leaders were in the East, the states granting suffrage were in the West. Suffrage victories were heralded in Colorado (1893), Idaho (1896), and Utah (1896).

The Woman's Bible

Chapter. II,

by Elizabeth Cady Stanton

Genesis II 21 - 25

> 21 And the LORD God caused a deep sleep to fall upon Adam, and he slept; and he took one of his ribs, and closed up the flesh instead thereof;
> 22 And the rib, which the LORD God had taken from man, made he a woman, and brought her unto the man.
> 23 And Adam said, This is now bone of my bones, and flesh of my flesh: she shall be called Woman, because she was taken out of man.
> 24 Therefore shall a man leave his father and his mother, and shall cleave unto his wife; and they shall be one flesh.
> 25 And they were both naked, the man and his wife, and were not ashamed.

As the account of the creation in the first chapter, is in harmony with science, common sense, and the experience of mankind in natural laws, the enquiry naturally arises, why should there be two contradictory accounts in the same book, of the same event? It is fair to infer that the second version, which is found in some form, in the different religions of all nations, is a mere allegory, symbolizing some mysterious conception of a

■ *Elizabeth Cady Stanton, a critic of church authority, drafted this feminist version of Genesis for publication in her 1895* Woman's Bible. *Her controversial views upset fellow NAWSA members, especially those formerly affiliated with the more conservative Stone-Blackwell wing of the movement, who preferred to focus only on voting rights.*

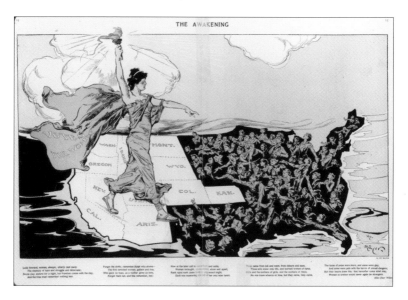

■ *"The Awakening," a cartoon by Hy Mayer published in* Puck, *represents the awakening desire of the nation's women for suffrage, advancing from the western states—many of which had already granted women the right to vote before 1915—to the outstretched arms of unenfranchised women in the East.* LC-USZC2-1206

Countless African American women's groups joined together in 1896 to form the National Association of Colored Women, led by Mary Church Terrell, an educator and suffrage supporter in Washington, DC. One of its founding member organizations was the Tuskegee Woman's Club, which had been formed the previous year by teacher Adella Hunt Logan and school administrator Margaret Murray Washington, Booker T. Washington's third wife.

■ *Adella Hunt Logan and her husband, Warren Logan (back row, second and third from left), pose on their Tuskegee front porch in December 1913 with six of their children, including daughter Ruth (back row, second from right) and son Paul (back row, far right), whose godmother was Emily Howland, a white northern suffragist who befriended and encouraged Adella when other whites did not.* PHOTOGRAPH BY ARTHUR P. BEDOU, NEW ORLEANS. COLLECTION OF ADELE LOGAN ALEXANDER, WASHINGTON, DC

OPENING STUDENTS' MINDS
ADELLA HUNT LOGAN (1863–1915), RUTH LOGAN ROBERTS (1891–1968), AND THE TUSKEGEE WOMAN'S CLUB

Adella Hunt Logan was born in Sparta, Georgia, to a white father and a free mulatto mother of part Indian ancestry. Her family's ties to upper-class white society provided her and her siblings a more comfortable life than most blacks and many whites enjoyed in the post–Civil War South. Encouraged by her illiterate mother, she attended college, started teaching at age sixteen, and later graduated from the Normal School at Atlanta University in 1881. Two years later, she joined the faculty of the recently founded Tuskegee Institute in Alabama.

Adella Hunt was a passionate instructor—teaching English and social studies, prepping the debate team, and urging students to become engaged in civic affairs. In 1888, she married Tuskegee's treasurer, Warren Logan, one of Booker T. Washington's most trusted colleagues, and together they had nine children in twenty years. Despite family obligations, she still taught intermittently and carefully championed women's suffrage in a state notoriously unsympathetic to it.

For ten years, Adella Hunt Logan was the only life member of the National American Woman Suffrage Association in Alabama, but she often had to pass as white just to attend the organization's segregated meetings. She withstood slights by national leaders, who dismissed her abilities or distanced themselves for fear of alienating white southern suffragists. Even at Tuskegee, Logan had to tread carefully because the conservative Washington hesitated to support women's suffrage publicly, believing that other issues were more important to blacks.

Logan agreed that blacks faced immense challenges, but she asked in 1905, "If white American women with all their natural and acquired advantages need the ballot . . . how much more do black Americans, male and female, need the strong defense of a vote?" She conducted monthly suffrage meetings for the Tuskegee Woman's Club, assembled an extensive lending library of suffrage publications, and organized events for students and local women, including a slide show that featured Sojourner Truth's role in the suffrage campaign. Prominent white reformers and black professionals often visited Washington, and Logan—who lived next door—used these opportunities to exchange ideas about women's suffrage.

When Tuskegee hosted a 1912 conference of black medical professionals, Logan's daughter Ruth, the school's new coordinator of women's physical education, organized a welcoming pageant that included a student "suffragette parade." That same year, Logan risked offending her friend Washington by publishing an important suffrage article in the Crisis, the NAACP journal edited by another friend, W. E. B. Du Bois, Washington's outspoken critic and rival. Although she had submitted articles to the Woman's Journal and other publications before, she had often done so anonymously.

From 1910 to 1913, Logan headed both the suffrage department and the rural department of the National Association of Colored Women. She encouraged the association's president, Mary Church Terrell, to resist efforts to keep black women from participating in the national suffrage parade in Washington, DC, in 1913.

In October 1915, Logan suffered an emotional breakdown, for which she was persuaded to seek treatment at a Michigan sanitarium by posing as a white patient. She abruptly left the clinic, however, when she learned that Booker T. Washington was dying, arriving at Tuskegee just hours before his death. Grieving for her friend and battling her own health and marital problems, Logan despaired over the recently defeated woman suffrage referendum in the state legislature. Her emotional

■ *Tuskegee Institute faculty, including nineteen women who may have been members of the Tuskegee Woman's Club, were photographed by Frances Benjamin Johnston in 1906. Andrew Carnegie, the white philanthropist who provided substantial financial support to the Alabama college, is seated at the right of Warren Logan, Tuskegee's treasurer.*

LC-USZ62-7818

state worsened, and on December 10, she jumped to her death from the top floor of a campus building.

Although Adella Logan did not live to see passage of the Nineteenth Amendment, she influenced many students and teachers at Tuskegee, including her own daughter Ruth Logan Roberts, a suffragist and later a Republican Party activist, whose home in Harlem became a gathering place for young black intellectuals.

California Campaign Edition

THE WESTERN WOMAN VOTER

VOL. I　　　　　SEATTLE, WASHINGTON. SEPTEMBER, 1911　　　　　NO. 9

COLLEGE GIRLS PUTTING UP SUFFRAGE POSTERS

WASHINGTON, last November, gave women the ballot by 20,000 majority---the largest majority ever given a suffrage amendment in the history of the world. Here's to a bigger majority in California on October 10!

California Next ! !

■ *College women in California plaster the side of a building with suffrage posters in advance of the successful October 1911 referendum extending the vote to women in the state, just one year after Washington State passed women's suffrage, leading to the establishment of a new Seattle-based newsletter, the* Western Woman Voter.

WHEN HARRIOT STANTON BLATCH returned to the United States in 1902 after living in England for many years, she bluntly noted that in New York "the suffrage movement . . . bored its adherents and repelled its opponents." She promptly founded the Equality League of Self-Supporting Women (later renamed the Women's Political Union) to bring more working-class women into the campaign. After attending the NAWSA convention of 1900, presided over by an eighty-year-old Susan B. Anthony, and noticing how few young women were there, Maud Wood Park organized the College Equal Suffrage League in 1906 with a classmate from Radcliffe College. M. Carey Thomas, president of Bryn Mawr College, became the league's president, and her companion Mary E. Garrett its finance chairman and treasurer. Soon there were chapters nationwide. American suffragists such as Carrie Chapman Catt helped found the International Woman Suffrage Alliance in 1902 and paid increasing attention to suffrage campaigns in other countries.

Blatch and others introduced militant street tactics characteristic of the British suffrage movement. Soon in New York, Philadelphia, and San Francisco, open-air meetings, outdoor parades, trolley and automobile tours, and election-day poll watches were carried out with an eye for generating publicity and attracting new recruits. The Women's Political Union held its first parade in New York City in 1910, and suffragists used the latest technologies—motion picture cameras, automobiles, and telephones—to advance their cause. They moved the discussion outdoors, challenging existing social conventions of women's place in public and commanding the attention of elected officials. In Lawrence, Massachusetts, Margaret Foley "made a balloon ascension and showered

■ *Margaret Foley* (right), *a milliner who belonged to the Hat Trimmers Union, and an unidentified woman distribute copies of the November 29, 1913, issue of the* Woman's Journal and Suffrage News, *published by NAWSA.* NWP RECORDS, MANUSCRIPT DIVISION

down rainbow literature upon an eager crowd." Others in the state "spoke in parks and pleasure resorts and outside the factories as well as in the streets and at one Yiddish and one French meeting."

The young film industry and daily newspapers documented the demonstrators' adept use of banners, posters, and costumes. Political

■ *Nora Blatch de Forest (1883–1971), a civil engineer and the granddaughter of Elizabeth Cady Stanton, assisted in her mother's efforts to appeal to women workers and their male supporters. In this broadside, she took aim at antisuffragist senator Elihu Root's contentions that the divine "duty" and "right of protection rests with the male," arguing that only through the vote could women workers protect themselves from exploitation.*

HARRIOT STANTON BLATCH PAPERS, MANUSCRIPT DIVISION. LC-MSS-12997-11

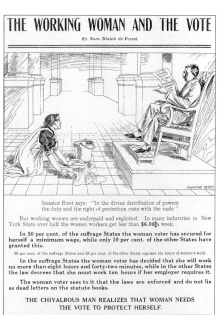

THE WORKING WOMAN AND THE VOTE
By Nora Blatch de Forest

Senator Root says: "In the divine distribution of powers the duty and the right of protection rests with the male."

But working women are underpaid and exploited. In many industries in New York State over half the women workers get less than **$6.00** a week.

In 50 per cent. of the suffrage States the woman voter has secured for herself a minimum wage, while only 10 per cent. of the other States have granted this.

60 per cent. of the suffrage States and 58 per cent. of the other States regulate the hours of women's work.

In the suffrage States the woman voter has decided that she will work no more than eight hours and forty-two minutes, while in the other States the law decrees that she must work ten hours if her employer requires it.

The woman voter sees to it that the laws are enforced and do not lie as dead letters on the statute books.

THE CHIVALROUS MAN REALIZES THAT WOMAN NEEDS THE VOTE TO PROTECT HERSELF.

VOTE FOR THE WOMAN SUFFRAGE AMENDMENT IN NOVEMBER, 1915.
JOIN THE WOMEN'S POLITICAL UNION, 25 WEST 45th STREET, NEW YORK. 25 cents initiation fee, no dues.
SUBSCRIBE TO THE WOMEN'S POLITICAL WORLD, 25 WEST 45th STREET, NEW YORK. Published semi-monthly, subscription price 50 cents per year.
This leaflet for sale at Women's Political Union headquarters. Price 10 cents per 100, postpaid 15 cents, or $1.00 per 1,000, express extra.

artwork, postcards, leaflets, and other publications appeared everywhere. Cartoons and broadsides questioned the domestic division of labor, obstacles to women's educational and professional development, and regulation of women's sexuality. They depicted suffrage as a means to end women's oppression and a safeguard against the corruption of male-dominated politics.

■ *Many early motion pictures depicted suffragists as pathetic spinsters or aggressive shrews who neglected their homes, browbeat their husbands, and ignored their children. To counter these images, suffragists began making their own films, including the 1915 melodrama* Your Girl and Mine, *which portrayed suffragists as sympathetic crusaders devoted to their families and to fighting political corruption.*

NAWSA RECORDS, MANUSCRIPT DIVISION. LC-MSS-34132-9

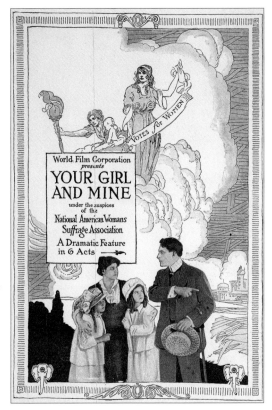

■ *Recently divorced, Nora Blatch de Forest devoted even more time to helping her mother, Harriot Stanton Blatch (1856–1940), on a campaign of parades, meetings, and suffrage publicity stunts in New York. Astride her horse "Senator Root," she joined Harriet Porritt on "Dr. Parkhurst" (left) to lead the Horseback Crusade for Suffrage in Orange and Sullivan Counties in August 1913. Both horses were named after leading New York antisuffragists.* HARRIOT STANTON BLATCH PAPERS, MANUSCRIPT DIVISION. LC-MSS-12997-20

■ *The cartoon "Spring House Cleaning—Why Not?," by W. H. D. Koerner, was published in the Wilmington, Delaware,* Evening Journal *in 1914. Women's suffrage was associated with reform designed to wipe out prostitution, gambling, and drunkenness.*

DIGITAL ID: acd 2a09997

■ *Challenging stereotypes about women's place in public, Harriot Stanton Blatch organized New York City's first suffrage parade on May 21, 1910. Each year the parade grew larger; here, on May 3, 1913, ten thousand women, many dressed in white, march up Fifth Avenue.*

HARRIOT STANTON BLATCH PAPERS, MANUSCRIPT DIVISION. LC-MSS-12997-2

Also promoting new confrontational strategies were Alice Paul and Lucy Burns, both of whom had traveled for postgraduate studies to Europe, where they ended up working alongside militant British suffragists Emmeline and Christabel Pankhurst in their controversial campaign. Both Americans were arrested for their activities, jailed, and painfully force-fed during hunger strikes in prison before returning to the United States.

In late 1912, Paul and Burns sought appointments on NAWSA's lethargic congressional committee to work toward a federal suffrage amendment. Within months, they had organized a massive national suffrage parade, modeled on the elaborate pageants held in Britain and the local marches in New York. The March 3, 1913, parade coincided with President Woodrow Wilson's inauguration and put the president-elect and Congress on notice that NAWSA would hold the Democratic Party responsible if it failed to pass a women's suffrage amendment.

Bands, floats, and more than five thousand marchers participated, representing nearly every state and most occupations. Crowds of men mobbed the streets, some of them threatening or injuring the women, while the police failed to intervene. Government clerks asked for a half-day off so they could march. Mary Church Terrell encouraged the participation of the National Association of Colored Women, despite pressure from some southern white suffragists to segregate blacks or ban their involvement. African American journalist Ida B. Wells-Barnett made a point of marching with her state contingent from Illinois.

Despite the publicity such events generated, Anna Howard Shaw and

■ *Born in New Jersey, National Woman's Party founder Alice Paul (1885–1977) attended Swarthmore College, as did her Quaker mother. She was a great admirer of Lucretia Mott and Susan B. Anthony, both Quakers who preceded her in the pursuit of women's suffrage.* NWP RECORDS, MANUSCRIPT DIVISION

■ *On March 3, 1913, the day before Woodrow Wilson's inaugural parade, an elaborate suffrage parade organized by Alice Paul and Lucy Burns for NAWSA received wide publicity, not only for its costumes, floats, and tableaux vivants, but also for the failure of the Washington, DC, police to control the crowds of men who gathered to watch.*

NAWSA RECORDS, MANUSCRIPT DIVISION. LC-MSS-34132-3

later Carrie Chapman Catt, as presidents of NAWSA, were fearful that militant tactics would endanger state victories, antagonize Congress, and make it difficult to gain wide support for ratification should they succeed in getting a federal amendment passed. Paul, who refused to yield, was dismissed, but she pursued her agenda through the Congressional Union for Woman Suffrage, which later became known as the National Woman's Party (NWP). Although their goals and strategies often differed, both NAWSA and the NWP engaged in carefully targeted but extensive lobbying of Congress and periodic meetings with the president.

■ *On the Coney Island beach in New York, suffragists wearing sandwich boards advertised for women's right to vote, probably in 1913.* HARRIOT STANTON BLATCH PAPERS, MANUSCRIPT DIVISION. LC-MSS-12997-8

■ *Elsa Ueland (1888–1980), who founded the University of Minnesota College Equal Suffrage League in 1907, worked as a Congressional Union organizer. Her mother, Clara Ueland (1860–1927), organized the Equal Suffrage Association of Minneapolis and endorsed Carrie Chapman Catt's nonmilitant tactics, whereas Elsa eagerly followed Alice Paul's lead.*

NWP RECORDS, MANUSCRIPT DIVISION

■ *Sara Bard Field* (left) *described her Swedish immigrant companions—Maria Kindberg* (center) *and Ingeborg Kindstedt from Rhode Island, who owned, operated, and repaired their vehicle— as "rather grim-looking."*

SELLING SUFFRAGE WEST TO EAST
SARA BARD FIELD (1882–1974)

Born in Cincinnati, Sara Bard Field was named for her paternal grandmother,
whose family had moved to Ohio from New York. Her father's family were
Baptists, a religion that shaped her early life, and her mother's family were Rhode
Island Quakers. Field attended high school in Detroit and in 1900—after her father
forbade her to study at the University of Michigan—married a Baptist minister nineteen years her senior and left for a church in Rangoon, Burma. Injuries sustained in
childbirth forced Field to return to the United States with her husband, Albert
Ehrgott, and their infant son.

Their daughter, Katherine, was born in Cleveland, where Field became influenced by liberal thinkers such as Clarence Darrow and Eugene Debs and grew
increasingly unhappy with her role as a minister's wife. In 1910 the family of four
moved to Portland, Oregon. There, Field joined the College Equal Suffrage League,
meeting both young suffragists and Abigail Scott Duniway, who had worked on
countless campaigns, each of which failed in turn. Duniway was eager to enlist the
aid of younger women.

In Portland, Clarence Darrow introduced Field to the poet-lawyer Charles
Erskine Scott Wood, with whom she fell in love. Realizing that she needed to become
financially independent of her husband, she took a paying job with the College
Equal Suffrage League, running the 1912 campaign for suffrage in Oregon. After
Oregon women won the right to vote, she went to Nevada, taking her daughter with
her. Working for suffrage there in 1913–1914, Field met Mabel Vernon, who introduced her to the Congressional Union and its idea of focusing on a federal suffrage
amendment.

When the Panama-Pacific International Exposition opened in San Francisco in February 1915, the Congressional Union hung a giant petition for suffrage and gathered signatures. The petition would be driven cross-country and presented to President Woodrow Wilson in Washington, DC, by the suffragists. When Alice Paul asked for help, it was difficult to refuse, so Field suddenly found herself setting off from San Francisco with two Swedish women in their newly purchased Overland automobile, driving from town to town and giving speeches about suffrage successes in the West. Mabel Vernon went ahead by train and made arrangements for them, an exhausting feat in itself. When they became stuck in the mud driving across Kansas, a farmer hauled the car out with the help of two workhorses, and on they went to New York, Boston, and Washington.

After the much-publicized trip, Field continued to work for the National Woman's Party in California. Her final suffrage activity occurred in February 1921, when she traveled again to Washington with Katherine, then fifteen years old, to speak at the presentation of the memorial sculpture of three suffrage leaders, Stanton, Anthony, and Mott, designed for the Capitol rotunda. Although Katherine was too young to have participated in the suffrage campaign, she, like other suffrage daughters, wrote about her mother's accomplishments and inherited her eagerness to support civil liberties and liberal causes.

■ Over the decades, many American women lobbied and petitioned Congress, first for the abolition of slavery and then for women's suffrage. Boardman Robinson's political cartoon, published in the New York Tribune, May 16, 1913, shows the polite reception these women received—but it also suggests the lack of effective action taken by representatives, who were not dependent on women's votes.

HARRIOT STANTON BLATCH PAPERS, MANUSCRIPT DIVISION. LC-MSS-12997-19

A RESPECTFUL SALUTATION.

■ *When Sara Bard Field returned to Washington in February 1921 for the dedication of a suffrage memorial at the Capitol, she traveled by train instead of automobile and brought her fifteen-year-old daughter, Katherine, with her. Here Katherine Field Caldwell stands in front of NWP headquarters holding the final issue of the Suffragist.*

NWP RECORDS,
MANUSCRIPT DIVISION

BY LATE 1916, Carrie Chapman Catt had resumed the presidency of NAWSA and recognized that the group's state-by-state strategy was taking too long. A brilliant strategist, she unveiled her secret "winning plan," a two-pronged attack that called for the careful coordination of state work with an aggressive nonpartisan lobbying effort in Washington for a federal amendment. By the end of 1916, both NAWSA and the NWP were working toward the federal amendment.

Catt's winning plan paid scant attention to suffrage campaigns in states she considered beyond hope, which by this time included much of the South. That had not always been the case. For most of the 1890s and early 1900s, NAWSA poured vast resources into southern suffrage work, believing that the region's racial problems could be used to secure votes for women. Directing this campaign was longtime Kentucky suffragist Laura Clay—the "Susan B. Anthony of the South."

■ *NWP members picketing in Chicago, where Woodrow Wilson was speaking on October 20, 1916. Both African American and white women participated.*

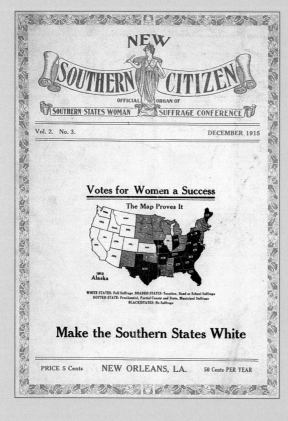

NEW

SOUTHERN CITIZEN

OFFICIAL ORGAN OF

SOUTHERN STATES WOMAN SUFFRAGE CONFERENCE

Vol. 2. No. 3.   DECEMBER 1915

Votes for Women a Success

The Map Proves It

1913
Alaska

WHITE STATES: Full Suffrage SHADED STATES: Taxation, Bond or School Suffrage
DOTTED STATE: Presidential, Partial County and State, Municipal Suffrage
BLACK STATES: No Suffrage

Make the Southern States White

PRICE 5 Cents   **NEW ORLEANS, LA.**   50 Cents PER YEAR

■ *The holiday border gracing the December 1915 issue of the* New Southern Citizen *provides a jarring contrast to the seemingly racist heading "Make the Southern States White," a widely repeated slogan appearing under a US map showing, in white, those states which had passed legislation granting women full suffrage.*

Bringing In the South
The Clay Family of Kentucky

The foremost southern white suffragist, Laura Clay believed that God had called her to take up the suffrage cause, but her parents' divorce and the family's reform politics likely played key roles as well. She was born in Lexington, Kentucky, in 1849, the third daughter of Mary Jane Warfield Clay and antislavery newspaper editor Cassius Marcellus Clay, who was appointed ambassador to Russia in 1861. In 1878 a philandering Cassius divorced Mary Jane, depriving her of any claims to the land on which she had lived for many years and had managed profitably during her husband's long absences. The divorce profoundly influenced all the Clay women and left Laura "unblinded to the . . . unworthy position of women."

Within a year, the eldest daughter, Mary Barr Clay—herself a divorced mother—attended the National Woman Suffrage Association (NWSA) convention in St. Louis, where she met Susan B. Anthony and arranged for her to tour Kentucky. Inspired by Anthony's visit, Mary Jane Clay formed a small suffrage club, and she and her daughter Mary began collecting signatures for their first of many suffrage petitions. Laura, attending the University of Michigan, was kept apprised through letters, while her youngest sister, Annie, attended their mother's meetings and later became attracted to Victoria Woodhull's controversial Equal Rights Party. Mary cautioned Annie about endangering her reputation and advised, "Let's work with them, when we think best, without connecting ourselves to the party." In fact, the Clay women never aligned themselves permanently with any wing of the suffrage movement. Mary Barr Clay and her sister Sallie Clay Bennett attended meetings of the American Woman Suffrage Association, of which Mary became president in 1883, but the very next year, Mary spoke at the NWSA convention.

In 1881, Laura Clay returned to Kentucky and assumed the presidency of the new Kentucky Woman Suffrage Association. In 1892, she warned the leaders of the recently merged National American Woman Suffrage Association that they would fail "unless [they] bring in the South." She became chair of NAWSA's southern committee and later chair of the membership committee, tripling the number of members and establishing associations in nine southern states. A tireless organizer, Clay found the work energizing, declaring, "I am in my element."

At Clay's suggestion, both Anthony and Catt toured the South and moved the 1895 NAWSA convention from Washington to Atlanta. Black suffragists, including Adella Hunt Logan, were discouraged from attending. NAWSA had embraced the "expediency" strategy, believing that white southern men would enfranchise women to offset black men's votes. In exchange, white suffragists were willing to accept literacy qualifications to eliminate uneducated voters of both races and sexes. By 1906, it became clear to NAWSA, however, that southern Democrats could restore white supremacy through intimidation and election fraud without giving votes to women.

Despite her continued affiliation with NAWSA, in 1913 Clay also joined the Southern States Woman Suffrage Conference, founded by Kate Gordon of Louisiana to promote state suffrage amendments and oppose federal action. When the Nineteenth Amendment passed Congress in 1919, Clay opposed it as an attack on states' rights and southern society. Ironically, at the end, she found herself standing alongside former antisuffragist foes in a futile effort to block ratification in Tennessee.

■ *Mary Barr Clay (1839–1924), photographed in 1883, became active in the American Woman Suffrage Association. Her mother described her as "a brave woman & one of the best electioneers . . . brimful of energy & hope, ready to do or dare anything."*

NWP RECORDS, MANUSCRIPT DIVISION.
LC-MSS-34355-39

■ *In 1916 Laura Clay (1849–1941) became president-at-large of the Southern States Woman Suffrage Conference. By 1920, when this photograph was taken, Clay had decided to oppose the ratification of the Nineteenth Amendment in favor of state laws granting suffrage.*

NAWSA RECORDS, MANUSCRIPT DIVISION.
LC-MSS-34132-4

IN JANUARY 1917, a dramatic shift occurred in the suffrage campaign when the National Woman's Party instituted the practice of picketing the White House. At first, President Wilson was tolerant of the pickets, waving to them as his car pulled through the gates. When the United States entered World War I in April, however, criticism of the government became less acceptable. The NWP did not support the war and did not halt its agitation. Other suffragists, however, stopped campaigning for the vote and devoted themselves to war work, including longtime pacifists such as Carrie Chapman Catt. Government officials found it increasingly difficult to refuse the vote to women who were contributing so much to the war effort, and antisuffragist arguments about women's mental and physical inferiority were difficult to sustain given women's war activities.

■ *Suffragist Mary Dubrow, a former New Jersey teacher who would later be arrested for her role in a watch fire demonstration, addresses a crowd, which includes children and a baby in a carriage, in Lafayette Park near the White House, c. 1917.*

■ *Carrying banners representing their state, profession, or local suffrage organization, women assemble on March 4, 1917, for the Grand Picket, when more than one thousand suffragists marched around the White House for several hours in an icy, driving rain, waiting in vain to present a series of resolutions to President Woodrow Wilson on the eve of his second inauguration.* NWP RECORDS, MANUSCRIPT DIVISION

The NWP highlighted the government's hypocrisy of supporting democracy abroad while denying half of its own citizenry the right to vote.

Beginning in June 1917, suffragists were arrested for picketing—the technical charge was obstructing traffic—imprisoned, and sometimes even force-fed when they went on hunger strikes to protest being denied political prisoner status. Women of all classes risked their health and reputations by continuing to protest. The NWP made heroes of the suffrage prisoners, holding ceremonies in their honor and presenting them with commemorative pins. Women went out on publicity tours dressed in prison garb and talked about their experiences in prison.

■ *Lucy Burns (1879–1966) sits in a prison cell at the Occoquan Workhouse in Virginia, probably in November 1917, after she and other suffragists were arrested for picketing the White House. Burns was one of the first two picketers arrested on June 22, 1917, and she served more jail time during her six sentences than any other suffrage prisoner in Washington or Boston.*

■ *Virginia Arnold holds a banner that accuses President Wilson during World War I of not granting full democracy in this country while sending troops abroad to make self-government possible for the rest of the world. When such a banner was first displayed in August 1917, an angry mob attacked the picketers, destroyed the banner, and later fired a gun at*

NWP headquarters, while the police did little to intervene.

■ *A cartoon published in the* Brooklyn Magazine *on November 10, 1917, pays tribute to American women's contributions to the war effort, showing Uncle Sam embracing a nurse ("American Womanhood").* LC-USZ62-76018

■ *Police arrested National Woman's Party demonstrators outside the Senate Office Building in October 1918. With only fifty thousand members to NAWSA's two million, the NWP nevertheless effectively commanded the attention of politicians and the public.* NWP RECORDS, MANUSCRIPT DIVISION

■ *Attorney Sue Shelton White (1887–1943) and other members of the National Woman's Party at the 1920 Republican Convention in Chicago carried banners for Tennessee and Connecticut and a large sign accusing the Republican Party of defeating ratification of the Nineteenth Amendment in Delaware and blocking its ratification in Vermont and Connecticut.* Left to right: *Abby Scott Baker, Florence Taylor Marsh, Sue White, Elsie Hill, and Betty Gram.* NWP RECORDS, MANUSCRIPT DIVISION

We protest against the continued disfranchisement of women
For which the Republican party is now responsible.
The Republican party defeated ratification in Delaware.
The Republican party is blocking ratification in Vermont.
The Republican party is blocking ratification in Connecticut.
When will the Republican party stop blocking suffrage?

Catt, as president of NAWSA, publicly disassociated her organization from the "unladylike" behavior of the National Woman's Party. Fellow NAWSA member Margaret Clark, who worked in the Senate Office Building, described the demonstrators as "ugly, ordinary, and coarse looking." But these radical shock tactics, combined with persistent, low-key lobbying, eventually won President Wilson's endorsement of the Nineteenth Amendment and its passage in the House of Representatives in January 1918. Obstructionists from southern and eastern states delayed passage in the Senate until June 1919, while suffragists continued to lobby, picket, protest, and keep watch fires burning in front of the White House. Ratification by the states took an additional fourteen months of hard work.

Finally, on August 18, 1920, Harry Burn, a freshman Tennessee representative wearing the antisuffragist symbol, a red rose, shocked his constituents and the nation by casting a vote in favor of ratification. His vote gave suffragists their decisive thirty-sixth state. Burn later explained that he had in his pocket a note from his elderly suffragist mother, Febb King Ensminger Burn, telling him to "be a good boy" and support Mrs. Catt. Antisuffragists tried to overturn the vote, but after six more days of legal maneuvering, the governor signed the certificate and mailed it to Washington. The Nineteenth Amendment was officially signed into law on August 26, 1920, seventy-two years after women first demanded the vote at the Seneca Falls convention. ■

■ *After Tennessee ratified the Nineteenth Amendment—also known as the Susan B. Anthony amendment— Alice Paul unfurled the suffrage flag at NWP headquarters in Washington, DC.*

NWP RECORDS,
MANUSCRIPT DIVISION

CARRIE CHAPMAN CATT PAPERS, MANUSCRIPT DIVISION. LC-MSS-15404-3

■ *Carrie Chapman Catt arrived in New York on August 28, 1920, to represent the victorious suffragists after Tennessee ratified the Anthony amendment. She received a victory bouquet of flowers from Mrs. John Blair and was greeted by Governor Al Smith, Senator William M. Calder, Mary Garrett Hay, Mrs. Arthur Livermore, Harriet Taylor Upton, and Marjorie Shuler.*

RELATED RESOURCES AND SELECTED BIBLIOGRAPHY

The Library of Congress holds an amazing collection of suffrage material, including books, pamphlets, sheet music, motion pictures, photographs, posters, newspapers, scrapbooks, personal papers of the principal leaders, and the records of the National American Woman Suffrage Association and its offshoot, the National Woman's Party. These materials are described in *American Women: A Library of Congress Guide for the Study of Women's History and Culture in the United States* (Washington, DC: Library of Congress, 2001). To access this resource online, along with other online Library resources related to women's suffrage, visit http://memory.loc.gov/ammem/ and follow the Women's History link.

The following is a limited selection of the many sources that were consulted in compiling this book.

Alexander, Adele Logan. "Adella Hunt Logan and the Tuskegee Woman's Club: Building a Foundation for Suffrage." In *Stepping Out of the Shadows: Alabama Women, 1819–1990,* ed. Mary Martha Thomas, 96–113. Tuscaloosa, AL: University of Alabama Press, 1995.

Baker, Jean H., ed. *Votes for Women: The Struggle for Suffrage Revisited.* New York: Oxford University Press, 2002.

Bausum, Ann. *With Courage and Cloth: Winning the Fight for a Woman's Right to Vote.* Washington, DC: National Geographic, 2004.

DuBois, Ellen Carol. *Harriot Stanton Blatch and the Winning of Woman Suffrage.* New Haven, CT: Yale University Press, 1997.

———. *Woman Suffrage and Women's Rights.* New York: New York University Press, 1998.

Ford, Linda G. *Iron-Jawed Angels: The Suffrage Militancy of the National Woman's Party, 1912–1920.* Lanham, MD: University Press of America, 1991.

James, Edward T., Janet Wilson James, and Paul S. Boyer, eds. *Notable American Women.* 3 vols. Cambridge, MA: Harvard University Press, 1971.

Knott, Claudia. "The Woman Suffrage Movement in Kentucky, 1879–1920." PhD diss., University of Kentucky, 1989. Ann Arbor: University Microfilms, 1990.

Lunardini, Christine A. *From Equal Suffrage to Equal Rights: Alice Paul and the National Woman's Party, 1910-1928.* New York: New York University, 1986.

Mead, Rebecca J. *How the Vote Was Won: Woman Suffrage in the Western United States, 1868–1914.* New York: New York University Press, 2004.

Merrill, Marlene Deahl, ed. *Growing Up in Boston's Gilded Age: The Journal of Alice Stone Blackwell, 1872–1874.* New Haven, CT: Yale University Press, 1990.

Million, Joelle. *Woman's Voice, Woman's Place: Lucy Stone and the Birth of the Woman's Rights Movement.* Westport, CT: Praeger, 2003.

Sheppard, Alice. *Cartooning for Suffrage.* Albuquerque: University of New Mexico Press, 1994.

Stanton, Elizabeth Cady, Susan B. Anthony, and Matilda Joslyn Gage, eds. *History of Woman Suffrage.* 6 vols. New York: Fowler & Wells, 1881–1922. Reprint, Salem, NH: Ayer, 1985.

Terborg-Penn, Rosalyn. *African-American Women in the Struggle for the Vote, 1850–1920.* Bloomington, IN: Indiana University Press, 1998.

Weatherford, Doris. *A History of the American Suffragist Movement.* Santa Barbara, CA: ABC-CLIO, 1998.

Wheeler, Marjorie Spruill. *New Women of the New South: The Leaders of the Woman Suffrage Movement in the Southern States.* New York: Oxford University Press, 1993.

———. *One Woman, One Vote: Rediscovering the Woman Suffrage Movement.* Troutdale, OR: NewSage Press, 1995.

———. *Votes for Women: The Woman Suffrage Movement in Tennessee, the South, and the Nation.* Knoxville: University of Tennessee Press, 1995.

ACKNOWLEDGMENTS

The authors wish to thank Amy Pastan, series editor, for her assistance and support on this project. Thanks also to photographers Lee Ewing and James R. Higgins for photography for the book and to Adele Alexander and Rosemary Fry Plakas for their help.

IMAGES

Reproduction numbers, when available, are given for all items in the collections of the Library of Congress. Unless otherwise noted, Library of Congress images are from the Prints and Photographs Division. To order reproductions, note the LC- number provided with the image; where no number exists, note the Library division and the title of the item. Images from the NWP records are available online at http://memory.loc.gov/ammem/collections/suffrage/nwp. Direct your request to:

> The Library of Congress
> Photoduplication Service
> Washington DC 20540-4570
> (202) 707-5640; www.loc.gov